SACRED INDIA

SACRED INDIA
Hinduism, Buddhism, and Jainism

Ann C. Boger and Joellen K. DeOreo

Published by The Cleveland Museum of Art
in Cooperation with Indiana University Press

Copyright© 1985 by The Cleveland Museum of Art
Design by William E. Ward
Edited by Jo Zuppan
Museum photography by Nicholas Hlobeczy
Map by Joseph L. Finizia
Typesetting by Typesetting Service, Inc.
Printing and binding by Lezius-Hiles Company
Front Cover: *Shiva Nataraja* (Figure 15).
Back Cover: *Buddha Calling on the Earth to Witness* (Figure 24).

Contents

Acknowledgements

The preparation of a book is never solely the work of those whose names appear on the title page. The generous assistance of many members of the Museum staff enabled us to present this work in its present form. We would particularly like to thank Evan H. Turner, Director, for his support; Stanislaw J. Czuma, Curator of Indian and Southeast Asian Art, for his invaluable direction and advice; and Rekha Morris, Research Assistant for *Kushan Sculpture: Images from Early India*, for her many sensitive suggestions. Special thanks also go to Marjorie Williams, Associate Curator of Education, and John Schloder, Assistant Curator of Education, whose suggestions greatly improved our text. Gratitude is also extended to Eleanor Scheifele, Photograph Librarian, and Georgina Gy. Toth, Associate Librarian for Reference, for facilitating our research; Jo Zuppan, Editor of Publications, for her thoughtful editing of the manuscript; William E. Ward, Chief Designer, for his design of the final product; and Nicholas Hlobeczy, Museum Photographer, for the photographs. Finally, a particular note of thanks goes to James A. Birch, Curator of the Department of Education, and Andrew T. Chakalis, Assistant Curator, Extensions Division, for their continuing support throughout this entire project.

Ann C. Boger
Joellen K. DeOreo

India of the Buddha

GANDHARA
PUNJAB
RAJPUTANA
Dehli
Mathura
Sravasti
Himalayas
NEPAL
Kathmandu
Kapilavastu
Kushinagara
Indus
Jamuna
Ganges
Ganges
Banaras
Rajagriha
BIHAR
Khajuraho
BENGAL
Sanchi
Calcutta
Udayagiri
Deogarh
GUJARAT
INDIA
Bombay
Elephanta
Bay of Bengal
Arabian Sea
Amaravati
Madras
Mamallapuram
Polonnaruwa
SRI
LANKA

Introduction

The Indian sub-continent extends south from the Asian continent into the Indian Ocean (see Map). At its northern border a long chain of mountains, dominated by the towering Himalayas, effectively seals it off from northeastern Asia. In the northwest, high mountain passes, such as the Khyber and Bolan, provide the only land routes into the sub-continent. The diverse geography and climate of this land between the Himalayas and the ocean varies from icy mountains to torrid jungles, from barren deserts to fertile river plains and dense rain forests. Because much of the sub-continent is hot and dry, water — the source of all life — is especially sacred. Three major river systems — the Indus, the Ganga-Yammuna, and the Brahmaputra — flow from the north, nourished by the melting snows of the Himalayas. The Deccan plateau and southern India, however, depend on the annual monsoons, from June to October, for moisture.

The successive waves of migrating peoples settling in India, as well as its varied climate and geography, contributed to the development of a rich and complex culture. Here three great Asian religions — Hinduism, Buddhism, and Jainism — evolved in the centuries before the time of Christ. The spiritual roots of these religions, however, reach far back in time to the Indus Valley civilization and the Vedic Period.

A highly advanced urban culture developed along the fertile flood plains of the Indus River about 2500-1500 BC. Abundant archaeological remains indicate that religious practices revolved around the worship of fertility deities — mother goddesses, phallic symbols, voluptuous *yakshis* (minor female fertility deities), and virile *yakshas* (their male counterparts). Animals were held in high esteem, perhaps even worshiped; serpents were revered as holy. Trees and certain locations, such as rivers, hills, ponds, and groves, were considered sacred.

This indigenous, Dravidian culture was overrun by the Aryans, who came through the mountain passes of northwestern India around 1500 BC into the Indus River valley from the Middle East and central Asia. Having a distinct language and religion, they settled their new homeland, over the centuries pushing southeastward into the fertile Ganges River basin. Aryan beliefs and ritual practices are recorded in India's oldest body of literature, known as the Vedas, which were composed over a thousand years. The Vedas provide the only substantial information about Aryan culture; consequently, this era (ca. 1500-500 BC) is often referred to as the Vedic Period. Aryan religion centered around the worship of a pantheon of strong male gods, personifying the forces of nature, to whom ritual offerings were made. The central cult practice was an elaborate fire sacrifice performed by the priests, or Brahmins. Aryan social and spiritual life were dominated by these Brahmins, whose religion has been called Brahmanism. Appearing early in the Vedas and reinforcing the authority of the Brahmins was the concept of a strict social order which has persisted up to modern times. Indian society was divided into four major classes, or castes, based on occupation: The *Brahmins*, or priests and sages; the *Kshatriyas*, or warriors and rulers; the *Vaishyas*, or merchants; and the *Shudras*, or laborers. All others were "outcaste."

Near the end of the Vedic Period, about the seventh-sixth centuries BC, certain fundamental concepts appeared which profoundly influenced later Indian thought. One of these was transmigration or reincarnation, the belief that the soul migrates through endless lives, being reborn in numerous animal and human forms. Inextricably linked with the concept of transmigration was the doctrine of karma, or deeds, which holds that the accumulation of good and evil conduct in a person's former lives somehow determines the quality of the lives to come. Karma was believed to operate as a natural law. These doctrines not only provided a religious foundation for the caste system, but also offered a reason for experiencing suffering in life. In time, it was believed that an individual's only hope for salvation — the union of the individual self with the universal spirit — came through breaking the cycle of rebirths.

The late Vedic Period also witnessed the appearance of a special class of holy men, besides the Brahmins. Finding Brahmanic rituals and sacrifices ineffective as a means of achieving spiritual salvation, these men, irrespective of caste, left their homes and duties in the secular world to become forest hermits or wanderers. Practicing various meditational techniques (yoga) and severe austerities (fasting, celibacy, solitude — the self-denial of all appetites), these ascetics sought to purify their minds and bodies to transcend the physical world and thereby achieve Perfect Knowledge. Asceticism and yoga have held an honored place in all indigenous Indian religions ever since.

Also during the late Vedic Period, the individual characters and qualities of the early Vedic gods began to be obscured or transformed by both the passage of time and the fusion of the Aryan and Dravidian cultures. Heterodox religious sects also emerged and challenged the authority of Brahmanism. The most successful were Buddhism and Jainism. The historical founders of the two religions — the Buddha Shakyamuni and Mahavira — lived and taught in the Ganges River basin during the sixth century BC. Both men came from the *Kshatriya* caste and left their homes to take up the ascetic life. Both the Buddha and Mahavira rejected the Vedas and the caste system of orthodox Brahmanism. Not concerned with gods and costly sacrifices, they taught a philosophy based on ethical behavior, providing a moral structure for a society experiencing the disintegration of its old tribal organi-

zations and the emergence of strong kingdoms and wealthy merchants. Eventually, Brahmanism lost its hold over the lower classes who were attracted to the teachings of Buddhism and Jainism.

By the third-second centuries BC, a religious fervor spread throughout India and popular devotional (*bhakti*) cults appeared, in which the worshiper directed an intense love to a personal god as the sole means to salvation. This alternative offered hope to those who, through their lowly social position, could not perform certain Brahmanic rituals — a situation condemning them to an almost endless series of rebirths — or who could not leave their families for the ascetic life required by Buddhism and Jainism.

A new religion, Hinduism, emerged, based on this devotionalism and worship of deities. Accepting the ancient Vedas as its sacred scriptures, early Hindu beliefs merged the powers of the Vedic gods with the legends of popular local deities and folk heroes. The curiously complex and often paradoxical personalities of the great Hindu gods resulted from this merger. The gradual exaltation of the fierce Vedic god Rudra into the powerful and terrifying Shiva of classical Hinduism is a notable example of this process. This rapidly developing devotional theism also affected the young Buddhist and Jain religions. In this context, during the first-second centuries AD, the first cult images were made for all three Indian religions to satisfy worshipers' needs.

In essence, then, Hinduism developed out of Brahmanism, and Buddhism and Jainism were essentially reactions against that religion. Although their approaches differ widely, to be sure, all three developed religions focus on achieving release from the endless cycle of earthly rebirths and gaining union with the Absolute — a transcendent reality with which man yearns to be united. For the less spiritually strong, comprehension of the ultimate reality which lies beyond the phenomenal world — the Absolute — is impossible. Indian religions, therefore, provide personalized gods equipped with a body of legends and myths, in which the devotee can place his faith, hoping to win a better place in his next life and move closer to the ultimate reintegration with the cosmos.

Over the centuries, Indian art has been committed to creating visual interpretations of these various gods and transcendental beings. The resulting images, however, are sometimes bewildering to Westerners. *Sacred India* presents some of the more popular imagery of Hinduism, Buddhism, and Jainism and explains their iconography and myths. Although we are likely to see these sculptures and paintings isolated in a museum setting, it is important to remember that they were not intended as works of art but as articles of devotion.

"The concern of Hindu, Buddhist and Jain art has always been the directing of men to union with the Great Beings that it reveals in tangible form. To that end no skill, nor time, nor patience could ever be too much. The works of art were guide posts to lead men by slow apprehension or sudden intuition to find the treasure hid in the shrine of their own hearts, the seat of the Buddha, of Vishnu, of Shiva."

Benjamin Rowland, *The Art and Achitecture of India: Buddhist, Hindu, Jain,* p. 357.

I The Dance of the God Within

When looking at Hindu art, Westerners are frequently baffled by the many-armed deities, some half animal, half human in appearance. These puzzling gods and goddesses in fact represent the concrete expressions of a complex, transcendent, and speculative philosophy.

In Hindu thought, the supreme divinity has no form or attributes and exists beyond time. This Absolute is the eternal source and substance of everything in the universe. The everyday world is transitory. Although great mountain ranges seem permanent and immovable, when viewed from the perspective of millennia, they rise and fall like waves. Measured against eternity, these same great ranges flicker and vanish like fleeting illusions. This illusory world is what we, with our limited human vision, perceive as changeless and real. This great deception of our senses flows from our restricted, self-centered consciousness; we are bewitched by the play of *maya* — the fluid, illusory, self-generated manifestations of the Absolute. To cut through this web of illusion and to merge with the unchanging reality beyond — the Absolute itself — is the ultimate Hindu aim.

Almost inconceivable — beyond form, time, and space — the Absolute cannot be represented visually. Some conception of the Divine, however, is necessary for most people, so Hinduism also has a Supreme Being, a god in a more personal form. Images of the Supreme Being provide temporary quarters for this neuter, omnipotent deity and serve as places where, through meditation or intense personal devotion, devotees may experience direct contact with the god. Such an image, which is thought of as a kind of metaphysical power terminal, is placed in the center of a small, dark, windowless room, the *garbhagriha*, or womb chamber, in a Hindu temple. In the example shown in Figure 1, the Supreme Being is represented abstractly in the form of a short, rounded pillar known

Figure 1. *Sanctuary of the Linga.*
Stone. India, Elephanta, Shiva Temple, 8th century.
Photo: Archaeological Survey of India.

as a *linga*. In a temple like the Kandariya Mahadeva at Khajuraho (Figure 2), the highest point of the roof is positioned over the *garbhagriha*. This vertical alignment of mountain peak (the main roof tower) and cave (the womb chamber containing the image) is believed to form an axis of cosmic power.

For those needing a more intimate god than this neuter, impersonal deity, the Supreme Being is further personified as a trinity. Each of the three deities has a particular, universal role: Brahma, the Creator; Vishnu, the Preserver; and Shiva, the Destroyer. These three aspects of the Supreme Being are illustrated in a small eighteenth-century painting depicting Vishvamitra, sitting in a yogic position (Figure 3). Although born a *Kshatriya*, he managed to become a Brahmin by practicing great self-deprivations. In this painting, four-faced Brahma sits on an open lotus near Vishvamitra's navel — a physical reminder of birth and creation and an important center of meditation. Vishnu the Preserver appears near Vishvamitra's throat, a second important meditative region. Since darkness characterizes the formless universe and Vishnu is also known as the Pervader, he is usually portrayed as being either black

or dark blue in color. At the meditative center of command — the middle of Vishvamitra's forehead — sits Shiva, his body smeared with the white ash associated with cremation grounds and funeral pyres.

In actual ritual and devotion, however, this well-known Hindu trinity — the *Trimurti* — is not observed. For various reasons (described below), Brahma is rarely worshiped. Vishnu and Shiva each encompass all the functions of Creation, Preservation, and Destruction as does Devi, Hinduism's Great Goddess. As manifestations of the Supreme Being, Vishnu, Shiva, and Devi not only share many traits but also have individual natures. Each is associated with particular myths and symbols that allow us to identify their images and begin to reveal — on a more comprehensible, human level — the Hindu view of the ultimate reality of the universe.

Figure 2. Kandariya Mahadeva Temple.
Stone. India, Khajuraho, Dedicated ca. 1000.
Photo: American Institute of Indian Studies.
The temple is dedicated to Shiva.

Brahma

"The moon was gendered from his mind, and from his eye the sun had birth."

Rig-Veda, x:90

According to Hindu myths the great cosmic drama of the universe's birth opens on a limitless expanse of water, representing the formless chaos of the Absolute. Asleep on these dark waters, the Supreme Being, the Lord of Maya (whose substance is undifferentiated from that of the water), stirs with the impulse to create. Ripples spread across the Cosmic Ocean. The troughs between the ripples encompass and define space, the first element. Since space — the ether — carries sound, it begins to resonate; this vibration raises air, the second element, in the form of a wind. As the wind expands through limitless space, it becomes more violent, whipping the waters of the Cosmic Ocean into a froth. This terrific elemental friction produces fire, the third element, which boils away some of the water, leaving a mighty void — the heaven of the as-yet-uncreated gods. Then, from the navel of his cosmic body, the Supreme Being puts forth a single golden lotus. As the thousand-petaled bloom opens, Brahma is revealed seated at its radiant center. Four-faced, controlling the four cardinal directions, Brahma completes the task of creating the known physical universe.

Time in this universe is measured in great cycles. Each world cycle is divided into four world ages, or *yugas*. One complete cycle of the four *yugas* com-

Figure 3. *Vishvamitra.*
Color on paper, $7^7/_8$ x $5^7/_{16}$ inches.
India, Punjab Hills, Basholi School, ca. 1700.
Edward L. Whittemore Fund CMA 66.27

19

Figure 4. *Brahma Hides Cowherds and Cattle in Cave and Flies Off.*
Color on paper, $7^7/_8$ x $5^7/_{16}$ inches.
India, Pahari, Basholi School, ca. 1760-65.
Gift of Mr. and Mrs. Edward B. Meyer CMA 65.335

The painting illustrates a story from the Bhagavata Purana (one of eighteen Ancient Stories, or *Puranas*, compilations of legends and religious instruction). Brahma wants to see more of the young Krishna's powers and so hides his cowherd (*gopa*) friends and their cattle. Being an incarnation of the god Vishnu, Krishna deduces that the disappearance is a trick of Brahma and so changes himself into replicas of the cowherds and cattle and returns to their village. This feat both reveals his power and allays the fears of the cowherds' families. After a year passes, Brahma professes admiration for Krishna and restores the real cattle and cowherds who have no memory of their captivity or the passage of time.

poses one *Mahayuga* (Great Age), or 4,320,000 years. One thousand *Mahayugas* constitute one *kalpa* — one day in the life of Brahma. At the end of Brahma's day — 4,320,000,000 years — the three worlds (earth, the heaven of the gods, and the netherworld of demons) are consumed by fire. The ensuing night of Brahma is as long as the day. When Brahma awakes once more, he refashions the world. These days and nights of Brahma follow one another for one hundred Brahma years of three hundred sixty days each. Then, not only the three worlds but also the universe, the gods, and Brahma himself will vanish in a fiery Great Cataclysm, to be reabsorbed into the undifferentiated

matter of the Absolute. After the passage of another Brahma century — 311,040,000,000,000 human years — a new Brahma will be born and the great cosmic cycle will begin again.

Brahma is usually depicted with multiple arms. In Hindu art, multiple limbs generally indicate divinity (the reality that lies beyond the world of appearance cannot be suggested by the image of a god resembling anything in the mundane world). Identifying representations of individual multi-armed deities mostly rests on recognizing the objects they hold, their attributes. Lotus-born Brahma usually carries one or several of the following things: a book (symbolizing the four Vedas, the earliest sacred texts of Hinduism), a water-pot (symbolic of the Cosmic Ocean from which all creation proceeds), a string of beads, or rosary (representing Time), or a scepter (an emblem of Power). In the Vishvamitra portrait (Figure 3), for example, Brahma carries books (the Vedas) in his two uppermost hands and a water-pot in his lower left hand. The only Hindu god consistently depicted with four heads (referring to the four Vedas as well as the four cardinal directions), Brahma is also the only one usually shown bearded with age, since the Brahma of our era is believed to be in the fifty-first year of his one-hundred-year life.

Frequently depicted standing or seated on a lotus, as a reminder of his role in the creation, Brahma is just as often shown riding an animal. Each major Hindu deity has a specific animal or bird vehicle which not only serves as transportation but also symbolizes his essential aspect in an animal guise. Brahma's vehicle is the wild goose, or gander, which can swim upon the waters, walk on the dry land, and soar into space without being bound to any one of those realms. It symbolizes the divine essence — the Absolute — which pervades all creation but is not tied to or concerned with the events of individual life. In the painting illustrated here (Figure 4), white-bearded Brahma carries two attributes, a book and a rosary, in his lower and upper left hands.

Although representations of Brahma are found in most temples and his name is invoked in rituals, he is rarely worshiped as a personification of the Supreme Being or the Absolute. In the creation myth recounted here, for example, he is seen as an agent of the Supreme Being — a subordinate god, or demiurge, who fashions the material world to order, much like a contractor. In Hindu mythology, Brahma is closely and exclusively associated with this positive act of creation and is never associated with cosmic destruction or any of the other darker aspects of the universal processes. The all-encompassing Absolute, however, is by nature paradoxical — dark *and* light, terrible *and* benign, creative *and* destructive. This ambivalence, which Brahma does not show, is essential to the Hindu concept of supreme divinity. Besides, if looked at only within the scheme of the Hindu trinity, Brahma has no relevance to our mundane world. Vishnu's responsibility as Preserver of the world continues, and Shiva's

work as its Destroyer is yet to come. Both of these divinities, therefore, inspire reverence and fear, but Brahma's work as creator has long been finished, so there is little occasion to take notice of him.

Vishnu

"You are the bluefly and the red-eyed parrot, the cloud pregnant with lightning. You are the seasons and the seas, the Beginningless, the Abiding Lord from whom the spheres are born."

Shvetashvatara Upanishad, IV:4

In the creation myth, Vishnu is the name given to the Supreme Being envisioned sleeping on the Cosmic Sea (Figure 5). His bed is made of the coils of the great serpent Ananta (the Endless) — sometimes named Sesha (the Remainder) — who symbolizes eternity. As Sesha the Remainder, the serpent represents the remnants of destroyed universes. This Nepalese sculpture (Figure 5), seemingly adrift in a sacred pond, exemplifies the image of the Supreme Being sleeping undisturbed through a night of Brahma.

The Lord of Maya, Vishnu (Figure 6), can be recognized primarily by the symbols he holds in his hands. They are many, since, as the Preserver of World Order, he is associated with many mythological events. Four attributes have primary importance, however: the discus, the conch shell, the mace, and the lotus. The discus (or the *sudarshana-chakra*, the wheel-beauteous-to-behold) is a flaming, sharp-edged weapon of immense destructive power. Capable of laying waste to entire cities and immolating hordes of demons, it

Figure 6. *Vishnu*.
Bronze, H. 8 inches. Nepal, ca 10th century.
Gift of Doris and Ed Miller CMA 74.55
Vishnu holds his discus and a small bottle of water in his upper hands, a conch shell in his lower left hand, and the world egg — the seed from which the universe will spring — in his lower right hand. The inscription on the base translates as "He who bears the conch shell."

Figure 5. *Vishnu Reclining on Ananta*.
Black granite. Nepal, Kathmandu, 8th or 9th century.
Photo: Archaeological Survey of India.
In his upper right hand Vishnu holds a discus, one of his major attributes. His upper left hand holds a mace and his lower left hand a conch shell, two of the other symbols peculiar to Vishnu.

symbolizes both Vishnu's role as the Defender of World Order and the Wheel of Time's never-ending cycles. It also serves as a reminder that the sharp, bright power of the mind is a formidable weapon against the demon of ignorance. The conch shell represents the origin of existence and is obviously connected with the waters in which it (and everything else, mythologically speaking) was born. In addition, like creation itself, it spirals outward in ever-increasing circles. When blown, it is believed to reproduce the first sound, that resonance of space produced by the first ripples spreading across the Cosmic Ocean. A

fearsome weapon, the mace symbolizes the power of knowledge, the source of all physical and mental powers. The small water bottle in the upper left hand of the bronze Vishnu (Figure 6) and the lotus in the lower left hand of Vishvamitra's Vishnu (Figure 3) obviously refer to his role in the creation myth. In all his images, Vishnu wears a high crown, or mitre.

Ananta (or Sesha) is Vishnu's vehicle when he is represented asleep on the Great Waters (Figure 5), but

Figure 7. *Varaha*.
Stone, H. 152 inches. India, Udayagiri, ca. 400.
Photo: Archaeological Survey of India.

Figure 8. *Varahi*.
Bronze, H. 8⁵/₁₆ inches. Nepal, ca. 14th century.
The Andrew R. and Martha Holding Jennings Fund CMA
78.70

in his active role as Preserver, he rides an eagle,
Garuda. Vishnu's use of both the eagle and the serpent
— seen as classic antagonists by many societies —
indicates his paradoxical nature as a personification of
the all-encompassing Absolute.

Although personifying the Absolute, Vishnu is
seen primarily as a kind god working continuously for
the world's welfare. As the Preserver, he descends into
our everyday world at crucial moments to act either as
a guide or the defender of world order. These *avatars*
(descents) of Vishnu are either total or partial incarnations of him on earth. Although countless stories of his
descents into the physical world exist, there are ten
major *avatars* of Vishnu in our current *Mahayuga*: (1)
The Fish (Matsya), (2) The Tortoise (Kurma), (3) The
Boar (Varaha), (4) The Man-lion (Narasimha), (5) The
Dwarf (Vamana), (6) Parashurama, (7) Rama, (8)
Krishna, (9) Buddha, and (10) Kalki, who is yet to
come. Each represents a separate story and several
are frequently depicted in Hindu art. In only the last six
is Vishnu represented as being totally human,
although occasionally Kalki is depicted with a horse's
head rather than being portrayed astride a horse.

A striking representation of one of Vishnu's
descents, a monumental stone sculpture in northern
India depicting the Boar *avatar* or Vishnu as Varaha

(Figure 7), illustrates the moment of the god's triumph
over the forces of chaos near the dawn of creation.
The newborn Earth (personified as a lovely young
woman) was drifting on the Cosmic Waters when she
was suddenly attacked by the Serpent of the Abyss

Figure 9. *Narasimha.*
Bronze, H. 21¾ inches. India, late Chola Period, ca. 13th century.
Gift of Dr. Norman Zaworski CMA 73.187

Brahma. This boon specified that the demon king could not be killed by day or night, by man or beast, either inside or outside his palace, or on the earth or in the skies. Thus protected, he terrorized the three worlds. His only worry was that his young son was a devotee of Vishnu. The demon king tried to discourage his son in his devotions and even resorted to torture, but the boy was neither swayed nor, miraculously, harmed by his father's violence. To save the boy and restore order to the three worlds, Vishnu took form as Narasimha (neither man nor beast) and entered a pillar of the porch of the demon's palace (which was therefore neither inside nor outside of the building). At twilight (neither day nor night) Narasimha burst forth from the pillar, seized the demon king, stretched him across his lap (which was neither on earth nor in the skies), and disemboweled him. In this image (Figure 9), Narasimha, his deed done, holds aloft the flaming discus of Vishnu.

The epic hero Krishna, who possesses a charming blend of human and divine qualities, is the best-known *avatar* of Vishnu. His advocacy of an intensely passionate love of God (*bhakti*) as the surest means of salvation guarantees his continuing popularity. According to legend, Krishna was born during the reign of Kamsa, the evil king of Mathura, an important city in northern India. A wise man had predicted that a son of Devaki (a female relative) would slay the cruel king, so Kamsa kept her captive and killed her first six children. The seventh, Balarama, was miraculously transferred to another woman's womb before his birth, and the eighth, Krishna, was secretly exchanged just after birth for the infant daughter of a cowherd. This exchange is illustrated at the bottom center of the painting *The Birth of Krishna* (Figure 10). Krishna grew up as a cowherd who amazed his friends and adopted family with his miraculous deeds (destroying various demons that King Kamsa sent to slay him), while

(the personification of chaos, Ananta in a negative role), who dragged her into the depths. She cried out for Vishnu to save her. Vishnu, hearing her desperate plea, assumed the form of a gigantic boar (a creature of the land who also delights in water and swamps) and plunged into the Cosmic Sea. He uplifted Earth on his monstrous tusks and restored her to her rightful place above the waters. In the Varaha relief (Figure 7), the tiny, feminine figure of Earth clinging to the tusks of the massive boar magnifies his heroic proportions. The curve of the multi-hooded Serpent of the Abyss bending away from the force of Varaha's stride emphasizes the power of his upward thrust.

A small bronze from Nepal (Figure 8) depicts Varahi, a female counterpart of Varaha. She is Varaha's *shakti*, his active energy personified. The symbols she holds may vary, but like Varaha, she always has the head of a boar. Here she holds a drinking bowl, a fish, and a serpent; her right foot rests on an open lotus.

Narasimha, the Man-lion, was Vishnu's fourth incarnation. As a reward for his austerities, a powerful demon king (Hiranyakashipu) had won a boon from

24

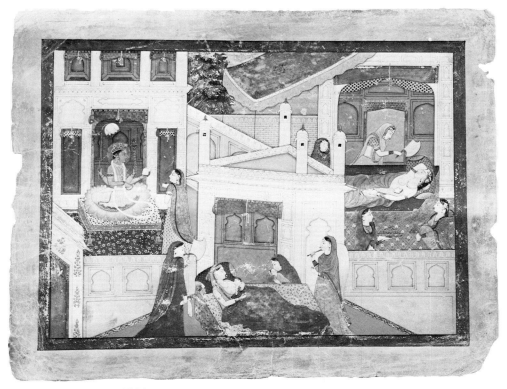

Figure 10. *The Birth of Krishna.*
Color on paper, 9⅞ x 13⅜ inches.
India, Punjab Hills, Kangra School, ca. 1800.
Edward L. Whittemore Fund CMA 53.13
The axe-shaped objects held by two of the female attendants are fans.

charming them with his beauty and amusing childhood pranks. Eventually, Krishna killed King Kamsa, and Balarama slew the evil king's brothers. Deposing tyrants and slaying demons occupied much of the rest of Krishna's life.

In art, Krishna is depicted as being dark in color, usually blue, like Vishnu. He wears a yellow *dhoti* (a wrapped and pleated piece of cloth), a low crown (usually adorned with peacock feathers), and many jewels. In the illustrated painting (Figure 10), he sits on an open lotus and holds Vishnu's emblems. He also wears the long flower garland frequently worn by Vishnu and which adorns Varaha in the sculptural depiction of Vishnu/Varaha's triumph (Figure 7).

Vishnu manifests himself through these *avatars* to defend the world against the forces of chaos. These struggles between good and evil, light and dark, go on through the endless *yugas*, the *Mahayugas*, the days and centuries of Brahma. The conflict has no ultimate resolution, but reflects the very dynamics of the cosmos.

At the end of a century of Brahma-time, Vishnu dissolves the universe and sleeps again on the Cosmic Waters. When he awakes, after another Brahma century, this benevolent Supreme Being will stir the Ocean of Chaos once more, put forth the thousand-petaled lotus of the demiurge Brahma, and the play of *maya* — the world we know — will begin anew.

25

Figure 11. *Ekamukhalinga.*
Black chlorite. H. 33 inches.
India, post-Gupta Period, 7th century.
John L. Severance Fund CMA 73.73
The *Ekamukha* prefix means one-faced. The unfinished lower half of the *linga* would have been buried in the earth when it was set in its original shrine.

Shiva

"I come as Time, the waster of the peoples, ready for that hour that ripens to their ruin...."

Bhagavad-Gita, XI:32

Unlike the benevolent Vishnu, whose relatively straightforward mythology emphasizes cohesion, existence, and light, Shiva belongs to the night, to all that is dark and mysterious. He represents dispersion, non-existence, and universal annihilation. He is Mahakala (Great Darkness), the eternal and measureless Time that ravages all things. But Shiva is a paradoxical god. What we see as the destruction wrought by Time is simply the natural, ever-occurring change in the physical universe, the play of *maya*. For one form to be created out of the formless stuff of the Absolute, another must change, fade away, die. Out of that death comes new life. As the agent of this change, Shiva the Destroyer is also the Creator. Within his nature all opposites are reconciled. Even his name indicates the paradox: Shiva means auspicious.

The form in which he is usually represented is similarly paradoxical. It is the *linga*, a simple rounded pillar sometimes adorned with one or several faces of the god (Figures 1 and 11). According to legend, in the awful darkness of a cosmic night of Brahma, Vishnu and Brahma began to argue about which of them truly created the three worlds. Suddenly, a great pillar of fire erupted from the Cosmic Ocean. Startled by this astounding cosmic phenomenon, Brahma transformed himself into a wild gander (his vehicle) and flew upwards, seeking the top of the pillar; Vishnu became a boar (Varaha) and plunged into the Cosmic Waters, seeking the fiery pillar's base. Neither could discover its limits. Exhausted and bewildered, the two gods finally returned to the ocean surface. As they discussed this mysterious and frightening phenomenon, the flaming pillar split open, revealing Shiva at its fiery heart. His thunderous laughter filled the cosmos, just as his pillar of fire illuminated the primordial darkness. Vishnu and Brahma bowed down before him, acknowledging Shiva as the ultimate reality. At the dawn of the next creation, Brahma placed a stone pillar on earth, the *linga* or sign of Shiva, to make Shiva Mahadeva — the Great God — accessible to man. The *linga*, the prime symbol of the Destroyer, the Lord of Death, is a phallic emblem, the embodiment of creation and life.

Whereas Vishnu manifests himself through *avatars*, Shiva manifests himself through personifications of his own powers. Since he is the all-powerful god in whom all opposites are reconciled, his different forms are numberless. Some general characteristics, however, remain constant. In paintings, for example, Shiva is always white, or ash-colored, as in the Vishvamitra portrait (Figure 3). Holding a rosary (Time), he sits on Vishvamitra's forehead, the meditative center of command, because he is Mahayogi, the supreme practitioner of that form of meditation known as yoga. He

Figure 12. *Ardhanarishvara Trident*.
Bronze, 15⁹/₁₆ inches. India, Chola Period, 11th-12th century.
Purchase from the J. H. Wade Fund CMA 69.117

has the long, matted hair of an ascetic, usually piled high on his head. As illustrated on the *Ekamukhalinga* (Figure 11), Shiva usually wears a crescent moon in his hair. The cup containing the elixir of immortality, the crescent moon symbolizes the unending cycles of Time and is associated only with Shiva, as is the vertical third eye on the god's forehead. This vertical eye of fire is the eye of higher perception; it looks mainly inward. The intensity of Shiva's divine meditation is so great that if the eye is directed outward, it flames forth with the fire of universal annihilation. That the Lord of Yoga — the supreme, celibate ascetic — should be represented by a phallic emblem again indicates Shiva's paradoxical, all-encompassing nature. The *linga* not only symbolizes procreative power (Shiva the Creator) but also sexual control. All sexual energy is directed inward, adding to the terrifying meditative fire of the Great Yogi.

The varied physical forms in which Shiva reveals himself are often ambiguous or contradictory. Since he is the totality of existence, he is creative *and* destructive, light *and* dark, erotic *and* ascetic, male *and* female. He is, for example, Shiva Ardhanarishvara (The Lord Whose Half Is Woman), as represented by the splendid bronze *Ardhanarishvara Trident* (Figure 12). The right half of Shiva's body is male. It is clad in a short *dhoti* and his matted hair is piled up in an ascetic's topknot. The left half is voluptuously female, clad in a long skirt and with hair arranged in the ascending tiers characteristic of his *shakti*, the female personification of his energy. She wears a circular earring. In his extended right hand, he displays a battle-ax (*parashu*), a frequent attribute (it is the weapon he gave to Parashurama, Vishnu's sixth *avatar*, who used it to destroy the army of his enemies). Ardhanarishvara leans on Shiva's vehicle, the great bull Nandi, a symbol of controlled virility. The trident itself is Shiva's awful weapon, comparable in power to Vish-

Figure 13. *Sadashiva*.
Stone, H. 214 inches. India, Elephanta, Shiva Temple, mid-6th century.
Photo: Archaeological Survey of India.
The central figure, Shiva Mahadeva, holds a citron in his damaged left hand. A fruit rich in seed, the citron is a symbol of fertility, and corresponds mythologically with Vishnu's World Egg.

nu's flaming wheel.

One famous image of Shiva resolves the male/female duality of Shiva Ardhanarishvara. It is a monumental stone relief of Sadashiva (Eternal Shiva) in the eighth-century Shiva Temple at Elephanta, an island in Bombay's harbor (Figure 13). At the left is a frowning, mustachioed male profile, Bhairava (Terrible), one of Shiva's awful manifestations. He wears a skull on the front of his elaborate headdress and serpents curled in his piled-up hair. In his hand he holds a serpent with a flaring hood. Shiva is frequently depicted wreathed in serpents since he, the Mahayogi, is their master: to the practitioner of yoga, the serpent represents the dormant energy coiled at the base of the spine. The yogi must tap this serpent power to attain the higher levels of meditation. At the right is a female profile, Uma (one of the names of Shiva's *shakti*), who wears a delicate jewel-encrusted crown. She carries a lotus, a life symbol, in her hand. In contrast, the central face (Mahadeva, the Great God, or Maheshvara, the Great Lord) is not specifically masculine or feminine. The high topknot of this genderless Shiva's hair is decorated with a crescent moon and encircled with an elaborate crown. This central face nullifies or resolves the opposites represented by the profiles. The whole is an image of Eternal Shiva, the Supreme Being, a personification of the all-encompassing Absolute.

The Worship of Shiva (Figure 14) represents a typical depiction of the god. Covered with white ash, he sits in a small pavilion with his *shakti* by his side. His long hair is pulled up in the ascetic's topknot and a crescent moon decorates his forehead. He wears a necklace of skulls (a reminder to us of his fearsome, destructive aspect) and serpents wreathe his body. In this painting, Shiva sits on a tiger skin (the tiger serves as the vehicle of his *shakti*, and symbolizes the power of Nature, which Shiva transcends), but he is frequently depicted wearing a tiger skin, either around his

Figure 14. *The Worship of Shiva.*
Color on paper, 10⁹/₁₆ x 7¹⁵/₁₆ inches.
India, Rajasthan, Bikaner School, 2nd quarter of the 18th century.
Gift of Dr. and Mrs. Sherman E. Lee CMA67.240
The scene at the top of the painting is puzzling. Perhaps the lady in the palace is seeking advice from the figure at the right, who has the appearance of a devoted follower of Shiva. He may have suggested worshiping Shiva as an answer to the lady's problems — hence the offerings to the god seated in the pavilion in the bottom half of the painting.

waist or across one shoulder. Shiva's trident stands upright nearby.

The most famous and evocative images of Shiva are those showing him as Nataraja, the Lord of Dance (Figure 15). These images give concrete expression to the Hindu idea of the endless motion and change of the physical world. We can perceive motion and change only through time; conversely, we know time only by observing motion and change. Dance *is* motion and change, through time. As such, it captures the essence of life. Shiva Mahakala (Great Darkness or Eternal Time) depicted as Nataraja, the Lord of Dance, represents the eternal energy behind the ceaseless flux of the cosmos. His dance sets matter in motion and sustains its movement and change. At the end of an aeon, Shiva's dance becomes horrifyingly violent:

Figure 15. *Shiva Nataraja.*
Copper, H. 43$7/8$ inches.
India, Chola Period, 11th century.
Purchase from the J.H. Wade Fund CMA 30.331

matter is flung apart and the universe ends in flames.

In this sculpture (Figure 15), Nataraja holds in his upper right hand an hourglass-shaped drum that beats the rhythm of his dance. The drum beats convey the sound of the resonating space at the dawn of creation; the drum, therefore, symbolizes life. In his upper left hand, Nataraja bears a tongue of fire, the agent of universal annihilation. Life and prosperity (the drum)

exist side by side with death and destruction (the flame) in Shiva's paradoxical nature, where all opposites are reconciled. His second right hand, for example, displays the fear-not gesture (*abhaya mudra*) of protection and peace, while his second left hand points downward to his uplifted foot, a symbol of Release, or total union with the Absolute. He dances on the body of a prostrate dwarf, who symbolizes human ignorance and forgetfulness. The ring of flames surrounding the Cosmic Dancer stands for the physical universe. It is a reminder that the great dance of Nature (life) is energized by the dance of the god within.

As Nataraja, Shiva with the moon in his crown represents Total Activity, the energy behind all motion and change; in other words, he is the Lord of Maya. As his impassive face indicates, however, Nataraja is also Mahayogi, who represents Total Tranquillity, the void of the Absolute in which all tensions relax. When fully comprehended, the image of Shiva as the Cosmic Dancer (Figure 15) reminds his devotees that any belief in the permanence of this world is foolish, and that by revealing this truth, he offers hope of Release.

Figure 16. *Shiva and Parvati.*
Bronze, 13⅜ x 9 inches.
India, Chola Period, 11th-12th century.
Purchase from the J. H. Wade Fund CMA 54.7
Poles would have been slipped through the rings on each side of the base so that the image could be carried in religious processions.

Devi

"O thou who hast the nature of all, Queen of all! O thou who possessest the might of all! From terrors save us, O goddess!"
Markandeya Purana, 91:22

In the mundane world females give birth. Since in Hindu thought, energy causes creation, it is logical that this Cosmic Energy should be thought of as female and be personified as Devi, or Mahadevi, the Great Goddess. As the personification of the energy behind all action, the Great Goddess is called by many names. When she is Brahma's *shakti* personified, she is known as his consort, Sarasvati; when she is Vishnu's *shakti* personified, she is depicted as his wife, Lakshmi. She is also Prithivi, the Earth, who was raised from the deep by Varaha (Figure 7), and Kundalini (the Coiled), the stored energy that must be tapped by

the serious practitioner of yoga. But the chief form of Mahadevi is that of Shiva's consort (Figure 14). As the *shakti* of this complex and mysterious deity, Mahadevi naturally has both benevolent and destructive aspects. In the form of the benevolent and divinely beautiful Uma (Peace of the Night), she won Shiva as her husband, seducing the Great Ascetic with the heat of her fierce meditation. Usually known as Parvati (Daughter of the Mountain) when she is depicted as Shiva's wife, she is the female half of Shiva Ardhanarishvara (Figure 12). There are also isolated figures of Parvati, but she most often appears at the side of her divine husband, as in the bronze sculpture *Shiva and Parvati* (Figure 16). Like the female side of the figure on the *Ardhanarishvara Trident* (Figure 12), this Parvati wears a long split skirt and many jewels, and has her hair arranged in ascending tiers. Voluptuous and divinely beautiful, she represents the ideal woman.

Mahadevi has several terrific or destructive aspects, but the two most frequently depicted are Durga (the Unassailable) and Kali (the Black One). Durga is the great warrior goddess, a violent demon slayer. She has fought many battles, but one of the most celebrated is her destruction of Mahisha, the great Demon Buffalo (Figure 17). By subjecting himself to a severely ascetic regimen, Mahisha had accumulated psychic energy of such intensity that its fiery heat attracted one of the higher gods. Drawn by the magic of the demon's yoga, the god was compelled to recognize his spiritual incandescence and to reward Mahisha's titanic effort by granting him whatever he wished. Then, possessed of unbelievable power, Mahisha routed the gods, seized the throne of heaven, and ruled in reckless tyranny over the entire universe.

Figure 17. *Durga Slaying the Demon Mahisha.*
Color on paper, 7^1/$_{16}$ x 9^1/$_4$ inches.
India, Punjab Hills, Basholi School, ca. 1700-1730.
Mr. and Mrs. William H. Marlatt Fund CMA 60.51

31

Led by Brahma, the lesser gods sought out Vishnu and Shiva and told them what had happened. Terribly angered, Vishnu and Shiva poured forth from their mouths the fiery heat of their energy. The other gods did the same. These wrathful fires combined in a single cloud of flame, and then took form as Durga, the *shakti* of the gods combined. Attracted by Durga's awful laughter, Mahisha and his demonic army drew near. A terrific battle ensued between the two opposing forces; then, Durga met Mahisha himself and the three worlds shook. She slew him, and the army of the Demon Buffalo perished. Figure 17 illustrates the climactic moment of the battle. It represents *Durga Mahishasuramardini*, the Unconquerable (Durga) crushing (*mardini*) the demon (*asura*) Buffalo (Mahisha). Mounted on her tiger vehicle, Durga has Shiva's eye of fire on her forehead and his crescent moon in her hair. She carries various weapons and attributes of the gods, including the mace and conch of Vishnu. The demon king tries to save himself by escaping from his buffalo form through the neck that has been severed by a blow from Durga's sword. But he is pinned by Durga's spear, and there will be no escape. The next moment will bring Mahisha's final decapitation. In the guise of the awesome Durga, the Great Goddess in her turn becomes the World Savior by playing her fierce and violent part in the ever-raging conflict between the demons and the gods; like Narasimha's victory and Varaha's triumph, this episode simply represents another battle in a continuing, eternal war.

Mahadevi's most gruesome form is that of Kali (the Black One), the feminine (or active) personification of relentless, devouring Time. Always black in color, for she represents the darkness of the abysmal void, Kali is depicted as an emaciated hag with fanglike teeth and a long, lolling tongue. She is most often shown fighting demons. Mythologically, she suddenly issued forth from Durga's body during that warrior goddess' fit of rage on the battlefield. The bloodthirsty, all-destroying Kali is usually depicted at the side of Durga, who rides on her tiger (or lion) vehicle. Kali moves beside her on foot, lapping the blood of fallen demons. In *Kali Attacking Nisumbha* (Figure 18), the Black One herself rides the tiger. Her necklace of corpses is unusual as she is more frequently depicted wearing a garland of skulls or severed heads. Other corpses serve as her earrings, and she wears a lion skin around her waist. Three of her hands are in the pointing pose used for warning or scolding someone; her fourth hand holds the massive trident with which she attacks the green-skinned demon Nisumbha during one of the battles in the eternal cosmic war.

Whether she is worshiped as Devi, Durga, Kali, or Parvati, to her devotees the Great Goddess is seen as the spark arousing the male gods to action. Shiva, for example, is seen as the Immovable Principle, indestructible, transcendent, and inert — the very stuff of the Absolute, visualized in myth as the cosmic darkness of the Ocean of Chaos during the Brahma century that lies between universes. Only when united with his *shakti* — his dynamic, creative half — can the Lord of Yoga become the Lord of Dance and the play of *maya* begin once more.

Figure 18. *Kali Attacking Nisumbha.*
Color on paper, $8^5/_8$ x $13^1/_8$ inches.
India, Pahari, Chamba idiom, late 18th century.
Edward L. Whittemore Fund CMA 68.44

Conclusion

The rich and varied mythological tales of Hinduism are meant to convey, in a popular, pictorial form, the underlying speculative philosophy of one of the world's ancient religions. The major gods and goddesses of Hinduism (along with hundreds of lesser gods, spirits, and local deities) are seen as stepping stones along the difficult path of transcendental knowledge which leads to the realization of, and union with, the Absolute. Since few people are spiritually capable of comprehending the sophisticated concept of a Reality without form, without attributes, and beyond time, Hinduism provides the assistance of the Supreme Being, who has form and attributes, and who exists in some fashion in time. This deity is further humanized into Vishnu, Shiva, or Devi. The selection of one of these major deities as a personal god remains an individual decision. Any one of the three can be thought of and worshiped as any monotheistic god would be; the other two can be thought of as second-ary aspects or manifestations. There is very little conflict between the followers of Vishnu, Shiva, and Devi, or between the devotees of these major gods and those of lesser deities, because of the pervasive Hindu belief that the ultimate godhead lies beyond the divisions of cult: the worship of any god leads inevitably to the same goal, as they are all aspects of the Divine. This is expressed directly in the early Hindu text, the *Song of God (Bhagavad Gita*, VII:21-22) when Krishna, speaking as the Supreme Being, explains:

It does not matter what deity a devotee chooses to worship. If he has faith, I make his faith unwavering. Endowed with the faith I give him, he worships that deity, and gets from it everything he prays for. In reality, I alone am the giver.

II In the Footsteps of the Buddha

In contrast to the mythic origins of Hinduism, Buddhist legends center on the life of a real person, its founder, Siddhartha Gautama. Born about 563 BC into the aristocratic warrior clan of the Shakyas, he lived and taught in northeastern India, the heartland of Indian civilization. At the age of twenty-nine, Gautama left his wife and son, renouncing his princely life to become a wandering holy man, searching for truth. Known as Shakyamuni (Sage of the Shakyas) or the Buddha (Enlightened One) by his followers, he spent the rest of his life as an itinerant preacher in the flourishing commercial cities of the Ganges River basin. He made many conversions there among all castes and eventually founded the first monastic order in India.

Soon after the historical Buddha's death, stories about his earthly activities circulated among the small monastic settlements in northern India. Initially, they were repeated orally from one generation of monks to the next, until a body of legends evolved, distinct from the Buddha's doctrine. These legends constituted a religious biography that was not only entertaining but was also an important spiritual model for the monks. In time, artists evolved didactic, pictorial imagery in the form of sculptured reliefs and painted murals to illustrate the older oral tradition. This artistic development seems to have occurred at about the same time that the Buddha's biography was first recorded.[1]

By the second century BC, illustrations of major episodes in the Buddha's life carved in stone decorated Buddhist monuments in central India, such as the Great Stupa at Sanchi (see Figure 29). The idea that the Buddha, having passed into Nirvana, was therefore without form and beyond time profoundly influenced early Buddhist art, resulting in a reluctance at first to depict him in human form. His presence was instead indicated with hallowed symbols. In this aniconic phase of Buddhist art, emblems were borrowed from ancient pre-Buddhist symbolism to represent the Buddha. Among the most common are the tree, wheel, funeral mound (stupa), throne, footprints, and pillar. By the first century AD, however, a human image of the Buddha replaced the symbols and biographical scenes were illustrated with great realism. This rich narrative art declined after the third century, when a new form of Buddhism, Mahayana Buddhism, focused worship on the Buddha as a transcendental divine being rather than as a historical person. Finally, large, iconic images of the Buddha were created in which only the hand gesture or posture indicates the sacred event.

Indian artists based their image of the Buddha on two ideal models: the yogi and the *Mahapurusha*, the primeval Great Man of ancient Indian myths. The yogi's supple, disciplined body was endowed with the auspicious bodily marks that characterized the Great Man. The Buddha is typically depicted either standing or sitting in the yogic pose of meditation, wearing a simple monastic robe, or *sanghati*. His body displays special physical features, or *lakshanas*, distinguishing him from ordinary mortals. The most frequently appearing signs of superiority include: (1) a cranial protuberance (*ushnisha*) symbolizing his supreme knowledge, (2) a tuft of hair between the eyebrows (*urna*), (3) hair arranged in short curls that turn to the right, (4) elongated, aristocratic earlobes, (5) three concentric folds in the neck, (6) webbed fingers and toes, and (7) wheel marks on the palms and the soles of his feet.

Hand gestures (*mudras*) give additional meaning to the image. The right hand held up conveys reassurance, and the left hand held down indicates the bestowing of charity. Both hands in the lap signify meditation, while the right hand extending over the legs to touch the ground is the gesture known as calling the Earth to witness. Both hands held in front of the chest with the thumbs and index fingers touching in a graceful circular gesture is the preaching *mudra*.

Ideally, the Buddha's face, the focus of the devotee's meditation, expresses the inner experience of Enlightenment. Displaying a blend of spiritual dignity and sensuous charm, it radiates spiritual calm and sweet benevolence. The gaze of the half-closed eyes is directed inward, suggesting a profound understanding of the life-process, while the gently smiling mouth reveals the eternal bliss of Nirvana. Glowing with divine beauty, the Buddha's expression speaks of his gift to the world — his absolute compassion for all mankind.

The Four Main Events

Almost from the beginning, four episodes in the Buddha's career were singled out: the Buddha's Birth, his Enlightenment, his First Sermon, and his Death at the age of eighty. They became known as the Four Main Events. According to Buddhist scriptures, the Buddha himself emphasized the importance of these four episodes, advising the faithful to visit these sites to contemplate the events that took place there. In time, the cities associated with the events, located in the Ganges River basin, became favorite pilgrimage spots for Buddhists: Kapilavastu/Lumbini — where the Buddha was born; Bodhgaya — where he attained Enlightenment under a tree; Sarnath — where he preached the First Sermon; and Kushinagara — where he died. Eventually the Buddha's sacred career became closely associated with a sacred geography and "following in the footsteps of the Buddha" has been a popular act of devotion among faithful Buddhists ever since.

Birth

"Then one day by the king's permission the queen, having a great longing in her mind went ... into the garden Lumbini. As the queen supported herself by a bough which was heavy laden with the weight of flowers, the Bodhisattva suddenly came forth, ... and from the side of the queen, her son was born for the welfare of the world, without pain and without illness."

Buddha-Karita, p.5

Siddhartha Gautama, the historical Buddha, was born about 563 BC to the warrior King Suddhodhana and his wife, Queen Maya of the Shakya clan, whose kingdom was located in the Himalayan foothills between India and present-day Nepal. According to tradition, the conception and birth of Prince Siddhartha were miraculous events. The scriptures describe how Queen Maya conceived during a dream. Siddhartha, residing in the Tushita Heaven awaiting his final birth, assumed the form of a six-tusked, white elephant and descended to the queen's bedside, where he pierced the queen's right side with his tusk and entered her womb. In ancient, pre-Buddhist mythology, the white elephant was one of the emblems of a universal monarch, or *Chakravartin*. Consequently the Brahmins interpreted the queen's unusual dream to mean that she would give birth to a child destined to be a world ruler.

Nine months later, Queen Maya and her attendants journeyed to her parents' home to spend the period of her confinement. Not far from Kapilavastu, she was overcome with labor pains and stopped to rest in the Lumbini garden. As she stood in a grove of flowering trees, she grasped a tree branch and the baby was born miraculously from her right side. The Vedic gods Indra and Brahma immediately appeared to

Figure 19. *Birth of the Buddha.* Detail of Figure 21.

receive the newborn. The baby was then bathed by streams of water falling from heaven. According to some scriptural accounts, the miraculous child stood on the ground and took seven steps in the four cardinal directions, proclaiming "I am born for supreme knowledge, for the welfare of the world. This is my last birth."[2]

From the beginning, the Birth was portrayed in terms of ancient pre-Buddhist fertility symbolism which continued to be used for the Birth scene even after the introduction of an anthropomorphic Buddha figure. The pose of Queen Maya at the time of the Birth, with ankles crossed as she reaches overhead to grasp a flowering tree branch, was adopted from earlier fertility imagery. There was a widespread belief in ancient India that certain trees would not blossom unless stroked or gently kicked by the left foot of a beautiful maiden. This image of a young woman bringing a tree to life through her touch became a charming and frequently used motif in Indian art. Prior to the Christian era, sculptures of voluptuous, scantily-clad tree spirits (*yakshis*) — holding a branch of a flowering tree, as they wrap a leg around the trunk or stand with ankles crossed beneath it — were popular auspicious symbols of fecundity decorating the stone fences that encircled religious monuments. From the second century AD, Indian artists consistently depicted Queen Maya in scenes of the nativity, standing in a similar, alluring pose under a tree as she grasps a flowering bough.

The Birth and First Steps are illustrated in the top arched panel of a stone stele (Figure 19). In the center of the relief (now damaged), Queen Maya, supported by her sister Prajapati, serenely grasps a tree branch as the baby emerges from her right hip. At the left the god Indra prepares to catch the infant in a receiving blanket. The nude baby appears again, standing on the ground, to take his Seven Steps in the four cardinal directions. A female attendant stands to the right holding a bottle of water for the newborn's bath.

The nativity is treated later in a less narrative manner in a stone relief from the ninth century (Figure 20). In the center of the panel, Queen Maya clings to a bough of a flowering tree, recalling the traditional pose of a fertility deity or *yakshi.* On the left, the god Indra, wearing his customary cylindrical crown, holds the newborn baby, while on the right, a female deity carries a fly whisk and a water vessel.

Besides his Birth, episodes in Prince Siddhartha's life leading up to his decision at the age of twenty-nine to leave the secular world were favored themes. Siddhartha lived in Kapilavastu, the capital city of the Shakya kingdom, in an environment of comfort and pleasure suited to a *Kshatriya* prince. At the age of sixteen, he married the beautiful Yashodhara, who bore him a son Rahula. The life of luxury, however, did not bring happiness to Siddhartha. Haunted by what he saw to be great suffering common to all human existence — old age, illness, and death — he resolved to leave his family to become a wandering holy man in

Figure 20. *Birth of the Buddha.*
Black chlorite, 18⅛ x 10¾ inches.
India, Bengal, Pala Period, 10th Century.
John L. Severance Fund CMA 59.349

The concerned Yashodhara is unable to comfort her troubled husband, who, longing for the serenity of the spiritual life, ignores a musician playing a flute for a lively female dancer. In the third register, Siddhartha resolves to leave his family and become a wandering ascetic, a decision made late one night after the usual feasting and celebrating when everyone had fallen asleep. Disgusted with his life of sensual pleasure, Siddhartha ordered his groom to bring his horse. Here Siddhartha stands in the bedroom before his sleeping wife. On the right, the court ladies sleep on the floor. The prince turns to a servant, who pours water over his hand — the traditional giving-away ritual[3] — symbolizing that Siddhartha is giving away his princely life forever. On the left, the groom leads in his horse.

The scene in the bottom register (now damaged) depicts Siddhartha's nocturnal flight from the city to pursue his religious quest. This pivotal moment in the Buddha's life is customarily known as the Great Departure. The haloed prince sits astride his horse. To the right, the groom holds an umbrella, an emblem of royalty, over the prince's head as the city goddess of Kapilavastu looks on. At the left, the Bodhisattva Vajrapani, a frequent attendant of the Buddha during his religious career, holds his attribute, a stylized thunderbolt, and an unidentified male accompanies him.

Enlightenment

"Then Mara called to mind his own army, wishing to work the overthrow of the Shakya saint; and his followers swarmed round, wearing different arms and carrying arrows, trees, darts, clubs, and swords in their hands; ... Beholding in the first half of the night that battle of Mara and the bull of the Shakya race, the heavens did not shine and the earth shook and the (ten) regions of space flashed flames and roared."
Buddha-Karita, pp. 139-140

search of truth. Courtly scenes, depicting the hedonistic life led by Siddhartha and his wife before the prince's departure, were particularly popular. The palace scene in the first rectangular section of a stone relief (Figure 21) shows Prince Siddhartha, seated cross-legged on a low stool, surrounded by courtiers. Within the architectural setting of the second register, the royal couple is entertained by court performers.

Figure 21. *Stele with Scenes from the Life of the Buddha.*
Schist, 26¾ x 16¼ inches.
India, Gandhara, Kushan Period, 2nd century.
Gift of George P. Bickford CMA 58.474

After renouncing his family and comfortable life in Kapilavastu, Siddhartha cut his long, princely hair and put on a simple robe, the customary dress for holy men in his day. Now referred to as Shakyamuni, or Sage of the Shakyas, he traveled for six years throughout the region of the Ganges River basin seeking truth.

Initially, he studied the meditational techniques of prominent mendicant teachers. When this proved unsuccessful, he retired to the forest with five ascetic companions to practice severe austerities. Eventually, when fasting had reduced his body to a skeleton, Shakyamuni realized that extreme penance was useless and broke his fast. Determined to achieve supreme Enlightenment, he set out alone for the city of Bodhgaya. There Shakyamuni sat down in the cross-legged yogic position in the shade of a large pipal tree and resolved not to move until he had achieved his goal.

The tree under which Shakyamuni meditated became a devotional object as well as the symbol of Shakyamuni's supreme achievement — his Enlightenment. The sculpture illustrated in Figure 22 portrays the Bodhi Tree, with its characteristic heart-shaped pipal leaves, being worshiped by Indian nobles, offering flowers at the altar.

As Shakyamuni sat meditating under the tree, a dramatic conflict took place with Mara, Lord of Death and Desire. Afraid of losing his power over the world if Shakyamuni attained Enlightenment, Evil Mara launched a monumental assault on the meditating sage. First, Mara instructed his three daughters — Lust, Delight, and Thirst — to seduce Shakyamuni, but they failed even to distract him. Enraged, Mara next commanded his hideous army of demons and monsters to attack. A great battle raged through the day, but Shakyamuni, deep in meditation, remained oblivious. By nightfall, the Evil One's forces were vanquished. Shakyamuni achieved his victory not by physical strength or superior weapons, but by his unshakable, impenetrable concentration.

Abundantly portrayed in early Buddhist art, these military and sensual assaults heartened the monks also struggling to reject worldly temptations. Probably inspired by the detailed descriptions of the bizarre hordes that assailed Shakyamuni in the *Buddha-Karita*, artists delighted in portraying dramatic battle scenes, including the animal-headed beasts and other hideous demons described in the text. A lively depiction of Mara's army appears in a miniature ivory (Figure 23). A large immovable Shakyamuni is threatened by a delightfully bizarre army of demons trying to prevent the Enlightenment: two demons blow conch shells in his ears, while a third beats a drum; about his head, animal-faced goblins and other grotesque creatures

Figure 23. *Buddha Attacked by the Evil Forces of Mara.*
Ivory, $5^5/_{16}$ x $3^1/_2$ inches.
Kashmir, 8th century.
Purchase from the J. H. Wade Fund CMA 71.18

Figure 22. *Adoration of the Bodhi Tree.*
Stone, $31^1/_2$ x $16^1/_4$ inches.
India, Amaravati, Satavahana Period, 2nd century AD.
Purchase from the J. H. Wade Fund CMA 70.43

brandish their weapons. Mara's two seductive daughters, crowned and holding flowers, leer at Shakyamuni from both sides. All this distracting commotion is in vain, however; steadfast in his concentration, Shakyamuni touches the ground to summon the Earth Goddess to witness his final triumph over the Evil Mara and his forces.

Figure 24. *Buddha Calling on the Earth to Witness.*
Black chlorite, H. 37 inches.
India, Bengal, Pala Period, 9th century.
Dudley P. Allen Fund CMA 35.146

Shakyamuni's Enlightenment may be too abstract a concept to represent visually. For Buddhists, however, the single image of Shakyamuni — seated under the Bodhi tree, cross-legged in the lotus position with his left hand placed in his lap and his right hand extended toward the ground — came to indicate the moment of Enlightenment, or *Bodhi*: he was now a Buddha — an Enlightened Being. This hand gesture came to symbolize both the trials of the Buddha's Temptation and his ultimate achievement of Enlightenment. In a ninth-century sculpture of the Buddha seated in the classic yogic pose on an elaborate throne, both the earth-touching hand gesture and the leafy boughs of the Bodhi Tree indicate that the image represents the Enlightenment (Figure 24). In keeping with the beliefs of Mahayana Buddhism, however, this sculpture does not represent the sacred event as a unique incident in the life of the historical Shakyamuni; instead, the Enlightenment is viewed as a timeless, eternal event. This large, majestically enthroned Buddha with a flaming halo and attendant Buddhas suggests that Shakyamuni was a transcendental, Absolute God, rather than a historical person. Furthermore, the substitution of small Buddhas for the more colorful narrative figures of Mara's army creates a formal, hieratic trinity, a common compositional arrangement in Mahayana art.

First Sermon

"The omniscient lion of the Shakyas then caused all the assembly ... to turn the wheel of the law. 'These are the two extremes, O mendicants, in the self-control of the religious ascetic, — the one is devoted to the joys of desire, vulgar and common, and the other which is tormented by the excessive pursuit of self-inflicted pain in the mortification of the soul's corruptions, — these are the two extremes of the religious ascetic, each devoted to that which is unworthy and useless.'"

Buddha-Karita, p. 174

41

According to Buddhist scriptures, Shakyamuni spent several weeks after the Enlightenment meditating near the Bodhi Tree, considering what course to follow. Having acquired Supreme Wisdom, he could follow one of two paths: either enter Nirvana immediately or remain on earth and lead others to Enlightenment. At this point the god Brahma, fearing that the doctrine would be lost, intervened, persuading Shakyamuni to impart his knowledge to others for the benefit of all mankind. Shakyamuni then decided that the five ascetics who had practiced austerities with him should be his first audience. He left Bodhgaya and traveled to the city of Banaras on the Ganges River. In the Deer Park at Sarnath on the outskirts of Banaras, he encountered his former companions, living in a hermitage, and preached the First Sermon.[4]

Northern India was then spiritually dominated by Brahmanism, the religion of the priestly Brahmin caste, which was based on the philosophy, rituals, and sacrifices of the sacred literary texts of the Vedas. Although the Buddha rejected the authority of the Brahmin priests and their rituals as the sole means to salvation, his teachings were founded on the traditional Brahmanic concepts of transmigration (that the soul is subject to continuous rebirth) and karma (that one's acts in this life determine the next life). The Buddha taught that each person, irrespective of caste, could attain salvation through his own efforts. Based on common sense and a practical approach to modifying one's karma, the Buddha's doctrine gave hope for release from the endless cycle of rebirths. During a time when northern India was experiencing social and political change, as well as spiritual and intellectual ferment, the Buddha offered an alternative life style, the so-called Middle Way, based on moral conduct, self-discipline, and meditation. By the time of his death, his doctrine and monastic order were well established throughout northeastern India.

In early Buddhist works of art, the spoked wheel (*chakra*) served as the visual symbol for the Buddha's First Sermon, which was known as Setting the Wheel of the Law (Doctrine) in Motion. In time, the wheel came to represent the Buddhist doctrine. The symbol for the sun in ancient pre-Buddhist cosmology, the wheel also appears prominently in early Indian myths as one of the emblems of the World Sovereign (*Chakravartin*). The adoption of the wheel as a Buddhist symbol, known as the *dharmachakra* (*dharma* for doctrine or law), thus implies that the Buddha is the spiritual ruler of the world, and his doctrine prevails throughout the universe like the sun dominating the heavens. Eventually a special hand gesture made by the Buddha, known as the *dharmachakra-mudra*, came to represent the act of preaching the First Sermon. Both hands are positioned in front of the chest, as seen in Figure 25. Together the hands form a graceful circle symbolizing the rolling of a wheel.

For many centuries, Sarnath, the sacred site of the First Sermon, was not only a popular pilgrimage spot but also a prominent monastic center. At the end of the fifth century, Sarnath workshops produced many Buddhist icons whose elegant and idealized sculptural style became influential throughout India and Southeast Asia. Found in the excavation of Sarnath, *The Buddha Preaching the First Sermon* (Figure 25) is probably one of the most celebrated Buddhist sculptures in India. Significantly, this sculpture combines both an iconic image of the Buddha and an aniconic, or symbolic, representation of the First Sermon. Carved in high relief, a serene Buddha sits on a throne in the yogic lotus position, his hands posed in the gesture of Turning the Wheel of the Law. An aniconic scene of the same event appears carved on the base of the throne (now damaged). Here the Wheel of the Law is worshiped by five bald monks and two deer, who symbolize the Deer Park; a donor kneels on the left

Figure 26. *Seated Buddha Preaching.*
Bronze, $6^{7}/_{16}$ x $5^{1}/_{4}$ inches.
Nepal, 7th-8th century.
Gift of Mr. and Mrs. Ralph King CMA 63.264

accompanied by a dwarf. The chaste simplicity of the Buddha, dressed in an unpleated, transparent robe, contrasts with the ornate decoration of the throne, the band of lush lotus blossoms on the halo, and the lively celestial beings. The deliberate, abstract treatment of the image, heightened by the smooth, uninterrupted surfaces and balanced geometry of bodily forms, expresses visually the ideals of Mahayana Buddhism — the absolute perfection and spiritual grace of a supramundane being.

Indian aesthetic norms and iconography greatly influenced Buddhist art in other Asian countries. A small, bronze Nepalese Buddha, dating from the seventh or eighth century (Figure 26), recalls the late fifth-century Sarnath sculpture in its lithe proportions and suave modeling. The Buddha's hands (now partially damaged) form a variation of the preaching gesture. Seated on a high platform, the Buddha's legs extend down with feet firmly planted on the pedestal — a position commonly referred to as the European pose — instead of the usual lotus position.

Photo: Josephine Powell.

Figure 25. *The Buddha Preaching the First Sermon.*
Chunar sandstone, H. 63 inches.
India, Sarnath, Gupta Period, late 5th-early 6th century.
Museum of Archaeology, Sarnath, Utter Pradesh, India.

Death

"When the Blessed One died, the venerable Ananda, at the moment of his passing away from existence uttered this stanza:

> *'Then there was terror!*
> *Then stood the hair on end!*
> *When he endowed with every grace —*
> *The supreme Buddha — died!'"*

Maha-parinibbana Sutta, p. 118

During the rainy season of his eightieth year, near the city of Vesali, Shakyamuni was stricken ill. Although frail, he decided to make a final journey northward to the land of his birth, accompanied by his followers and the faithful disciple Ananda. When they approached the city of Kushinagara, in the kingdom of the Mallas, Shakyamuni was invited to eat at the house of Chunda, a blacksmith. According to tradition, Shakyamuni fell gravely ill after eating spoiled meat. Unable to walk into Kushinagara, he instructed Ananda to prepare a bed in a shady grove between two trees. During his final hours, he converted an ascetic named Subhadra and delivered a discourse to the monks. Finally Shakyamuni went into a deep trance and died. The Malla chieftans conducted his funeral and cremation. The ashes were distributed among the eight kingdoms where Shakyamuni had traveled and preached. His sacred remains were enshrined in stupas, which was the Indian custom of honoring their kings and great heroes.

Buddhists regard Shakyamuni's death as the last important event in his spiritual career. Known as the *Parinirvana*, it was his final death, with no ensuing rebirth. After a succession of many lives, Shakyamuni

Figure 27. *Parinirvana of the Buddha.*
Stone, H. 26³/₈ inches.
India, Gandhara, Kushan Period, late 2nd-early 3rd century.
Acc. no. 49.9.
Courtesy of the Freer Gallery of Art,
Smithsonian Institution, Washington, DC.

had entered Nirvana, a blissful state of non-existence, the final goal for every Buddhist. A stone sculpture illustrates the emotionally charged death scene (Figure 27). Behind the recumbent Buddha, four distraught turbaned nobles grimace and gesture. Withdrawn from this grieving, the hooded Subhadra, the Buddha's last convert, sits meditating in front of the bed; a tripod supports his water pouch, a common accessory of itinerant holy men. At the far left, the bald Kashyapa, one of the Buddha's prominent disciples, calmly explains the *Parinirvana* to a naked ascetic. The long-haired Bodhisattva Vajrapani, holding his attribute the

Figure 28. *Parinirvana of the Buddha.*
Granulite, L. 600 inches.
Sri Lanka, Gal Vihara, Polonnaruwa.
Photo: Daniel J. Silver.

thunderbolt, stands behind the holy men, his hand to his head in dismay. Even the tree spirit emerges from the leafy boughs to witness the great event.

In later Buddhism, the *Parinirvana* became the focus of a special cult that required a large-scale image of the departed Buddha in its ceremonies. Probably the most celebrated sculpture of the Death of the Buddha in all Asia is a figure of the recumbent Buddha in Sri Lanka (Figure 28). Dating from the twelfth century, the fifty-foot long granite image is one of a group of four colossal sculptures located at Gal Vihara, once part of a large monastery near Polonnaruwa. The sanctuary that originally housed the sculpture was destroyed. The austere simplicity of this enormous, single figure conveys an overwhelming impression of the eternal peace and serenity of Nirvana.

Although the Buddha's original funeral mounds no longer exist, they were the focus of intense devotion by early Buddhists. The relics enshrined within the mounds provided the initial spiritual impetus, but the stupa itself also became endowed with elaborate symbolism beyond its original funerary function.

The Great Stupa at Sanchi (Figure 29), dating to about the first century BC, is the classic example of this kind of monument in India, which in early Buddhism was viewed not only as a funeral mound but also as a diagram of the cosmos. The massive hemispherical dome, rising from a square or round base, symbolizes the dome of heaven, which encloses the World-Mountain in Indian mythology. On the crown, a railing encloses a thin mast, representing the summit of the world axis connecting earth and heaven. Above the dome, the mast supports flattened discs, or parasols, that symbolize the heavens of the gods. A fence surrounds the sacred area around the stupa. Its four towering gateways face the directions of the compass. Two flights of stairs ascend to a narrow processional path, encircling the base of the mound. Holy relics, buried in small containers deep within the mounds, were enshrined in these stupas.

The Great Stupa at Sanchi exhibits some of the finest carved reliefs in early Buddhist art of the aniconic phase. All the aniconic symbols representing the Buddha decorate the stone gateways, along with subject matter adopted from the popular nature cults, such as the fertility symbol of the *yakshi*-and-tree. The stupa itself symbolized the Death of the Buddha in early Buddhist art, and at Sanchi, for example, carvings illustrating a stupa surrounded by worshipers represent the *Parinirvana.*

45

Figure 29. *The Great Stupa at Sanchi.*
India, Sanchi, Madhya Pradesh, 3rd-1st century BC.
Photo: Josephine Powell.

The Bodhisattva

During the four hundred years following the Buddha's death, Buddhism remained an essentially monastic religion. This early form of Buddhism — called *Hinayana* (the Lesser Vehicle) or *Theravada* (the Doctrine of the Elders) — closely followed the Buddha's original teachings. It revered Shakyamuni as a great teacher and restricted salvation to those joining the monastic order. This intellectually austere faith attracted only those who could renounce the ordinary secular world to undergo the arduous self-discipline and strenuous meditation necessary for Enlightenment.

Around the first century AD, however, a new form

of Buddhism emerged, answering the emotional needs of the large lay community and competing with the popular devotional cults. Called *Mahayana* (the Greater Vehicle), it taught that Buddha Shakyamuni was a god and only one of many transcendental Buddhas who had previously taught the doctrine on earth. These Buddhas ruled over paradises into which devout Buddhists hoped to be reborn.

Mahayana Buddhism also promoted the belief in divine saviors, called Bodhisattvas — the beings (*sattvas*) destined for Enlightenment (*bodhi*). Described as divine beings who had given up their entrance into Nirvana in order to lead all sentient creatures to salvation, the Bodhisattvas were regarded as personifications of the Buddha's virtues. The active agents of the Buddhas, they dispense compassion in this world to all suffering souls. For the ordinary believer, Shakyamuni and other Buddhas of the Mahayana pantheon remained remote and unapproachable beings in Nirvana, but the compassionate Bodhisattvas' power to descend to the world of men to administer divine aid made them accessible to all.

From the beginning, Bodhisattvas were depicted wearing princely attire and jewelry, and were easily distinguished from the Buddha who was usually dressed in a simple monk's robe, or *sanghati*. The typical second-century Bodhisattva from northwest India was interpreted as a strong, imposing, worldly being dressed as an Indian noble. This *Bodhisattva* (Figure 30) — with his sharply carved contemporary dress, his impassive expression, and his heavy body — characteristically conveys a powerful, realistic presence rather than one of mercy and spirituality.

Among the divine Bodhisattvas, the most universally adored was Avalokiteshvara, whose name means the Lord Who Looks Down (with compassion). Popular devotion in Buddhist India centered eventually on Avalokiteshvara as a world savior, who it was

Figure 30. *Bodhisattva.*
Dark gray schist, H. 52$\frac{1}{8}$ inches.
India, Gandhara, Kushan Period, late 2nd century.
Purchase from the J. H. Wade Fund CMA 65.476

Figure 31. *Avalokiteshvara (Padmapani)*.
Bronze, H. 24 3/8 inches.
Nepal, ca. 12th century.
John L. Severance Fund CMA 76.3
"All conquering is the savior of the World
His Lotus hand stretched down in charity,
is dripping streams of nectar to assuage the thirsty spirits
of the dead.
His glorious face is bright with gathered moonlight
and his glance is soft
with that deep pity that he bears within."
Ratnakirti, trans. Daniel Ingalls in *Sanskrit Poetry,* p. 54

believed rescued souls from the cycle of rebirth. The most popular form of Avalokiteshvara after the fifth century was Padmapani (the Lotus Bearer), customarily depicted holding a lotus blossom. Generally the lotus was an emblem of purity, but here it symbolizes the god's power to rescue souls mired in human ignorance, leading them to the pure state of Enlightenment, just as the pure white lotus blossoms immaculately above muddy water.

Worship of the Bodhisattva Padmapani was intense in Nepal, where artists portrayed the god as an alluring young prince (Figure 31). Identified as Padmapani by his attributes — the lotus and the tiny seated image of a Buddha in his tiara — the god stands in a langorous *tribhanga* (thrice-bent) pose; his right hand extends forward in the gesture of offering charity. Padmapani wears the usual regal ornaments and a diaphanous *dhoti* clings sensuously to his legs. Exuding human tenderness and sympathy, the figure displays a certain feminine charm that is enhanced by the subtle modeling and warm glowing color of his seemingly soft flesh. Ideally a sculpture of Padmapani visually embodies the god's immeasurable compassion for all suffering souls trapped in the circle of transmigration.

Another popular Bodhisattva is Maitreya, the Buddha of the Future. His cult in early Buddhism even rivaled that of the historical Buddha Shakyamuni. Buddhists believed that Shakyamuni selected Maitreya as the next earthly Buddha. At some time in the distant future, Maitreya would descend to earth to preach the message of salvation for the last time. For now, Maitreya, as a Bodhisattva, rules over the Tushita Heaven awaiting his final birth in this world. Early worship of Maitreya was clearly based on his role as a messiah, and Indian Buddhists eagerly commissioned icons representing him as a Bodhisattva holding his attribute, a bottle containing the elixir of immortality.

In a twelfth-century sculpture from Bengal, Mai-

Figure 32. *Bodhisattva Maitreya.*
Silver, inlaid with turquoise, copper, brass, and gold;
gilt-bronze lotus, H. 12¾ inches.
India, Bengal, Pala Period, 12th century.
The Severance and Greta Millikin Purchase Fund CMA
82.48

treya, dressed in regal attire and jewels, can be identified by his attributes (Figure 32). The bottle is supported by a lotus blossom stem held in his left hand, while the stupa appears on his head between the jeweled tiara and the elaborately piled hair.

Conclusion

Although in Southeast Asia and the Far East, Mahayana Buddhism had wide appeal, Buddhism generally declined in popularity in India after the seventh century, challenged by the rise of devotional Hinduism and its powerful gods Vishnu and Shiva. The last stronghold of Buddhism was in eastern India, where it received royal support from Buddhist kings between the ninth and thirteenth centuries. Buddhism prospered at the great monastic centers in Bihar and Bengal. Although monks and priests from all over Asia flocked to these monasteries to study the various forms of Buddhism, the religion had by this time lost favor among common people in India. The Moslem invasion at the end of the twelfth century dealt the final blow. The wealthy monasteries made easy targets for the invading armies that looted and sacked them. With its center of power destroyed, its economic base obliterated, and its popularity among the lower classes usurped by the Hindu devotional cults, Buddhism ceased to exist in its homeland.

49

Notes

1. Although many literary versions of the Life of the Buddha have survived in India, Sri Lanka, and the Himalayan countries, no single text includes all the major episodes illustrated in Indian art. The Buddha's life was first recorded in fragmentary accounts in the Pali canon of the Hinayana school. The first individual biographies, however, did not appear until the Kushan Dynasty (1st-3rd century AD) and were written in Sanskrit. Of the Sanskrit biographies, the most beautifully and simply written is the *Buddha-Karita* (Acts of the Buddha), which was composed in the second century AD by Ashvaghosa, a poet, philosopher, and contemporary of Kushan Emperor Kanishka I. Although associated with Mahayana Buddhism, the account's simplicity and its general lack of supernatural events suggest that the *Buddha-Karita* was closer in spirit to the older Hinayana tradition that emphasized the humanity of the Buddha. Another crucial text is the *Maha-parinibbana Sutta* (The Sutra of the Great Decease) which gives the fullest description of the events leading up to the Buddha's death, his funeral, and cremation, and the distribution of his relics.

2. *Buddha-Karita*, p. 6.

3. The "giving-away" ritual is an old tradition in India. Water is poured over the hands of the donor, symbolizing that like the poured water which will never return to the bottle, the gift will never be returned to the giver.

4. The contents of Shakyamuni's First Sermon included the essential teachings of Buddhism: The Middle Way, the Four Noble Truths, and the Noble Eightfold Path. Shakyamuni's analysis of the human condition, which is contained in the Four Noble Truths, is often explained in terms of a physician's diagnosis of an illness and his prescription for a treatment to cure the disease. The Four Noble Truths are: (1) all life is suffering, (2) suffering is caused by desire, (3) elimination of suffering is achieved through cessation of desire, and (4) cessation of desire is achieved through following the Noble Eightfold Path. The correct manner of living as outlined in the Noble Eightfold Path is Right Views, Resolve, Speech, Conduct, Livelihood, Effort, Mindfulness, and Right Concentration. The Noble Eightfold Path, therefore, followed the Middle Way between two extreme life styles: excessive pleasure and self-indulgence, on the one hand, and excessive asceticism and penance on the other. Thus, Shakyamuni's message to the world stressed moderation in living, self-discipline, and meditation as the means for Enlightenment.

III Saints and Ascetics

"With all your might the ascetic's tortures undergo; conquer the stubborn causes of woe ... and thus cut through the stalk of rebirth."

Kalakacaryakatha, II:77*

The Jaina faith allows no place for the worship of a deity or a Buddha. No god created the universe — it has always existed. Although the Vedic (and Hindu) gods, with their own powers and personal idiosyncrasies, ensconced in their own heavens of delight, are admitted to exist, they can do nothing to help man learn about or attain union with the Absolute — or Nirvana, in Buddhist terminology. As in the teachings of Hinayana Buddhism — the form of Buddhism closest to Shakyamuni's original teachings — man's hope of Salvation rests entirely with man. Individually, we are the masters of our own destiny. Only we can extinguish our own *karma*; whether we attain Perfect Knowledge (Enlightenment) depends on us alone. No god can bestow it.

To followers of the Jaina faith, there is only one road to Salvation. It is the difficult and painful path of extreme asceticism, involving physical austerities, supression of the passions, disassociation from the physical world, and the complete renunciation of all action. Only this road leads toward Nirvana, or union with the Absolute. This harsh path includes the most extreme doctrine of non-violence (*ahimsa*) in Indian thought: monks carry small brooms to sweep the ground before they sit, to avoid harming some small creature, and will drink only thrice-filtered water. Laymen are prohibited from entering certain occupations, such as farming, in which they might cause injury or death to another living creature.

The gods are not as important as the twenty-four great Jaina teachers, the Tirthankaras, humans who have found the ford or path through the ocean of birth and rebirth. Each pathfinder is a *jina*, or conqueror, of the phenomenal world and the self, while their disciples are *Jainas* (followers or sons of the conqueror). As Perfect Men, the Tirthankaras have gained release from perpetual rebirth through self-discipline, meditation, and asceticism. After Enlightenment and before their final death and entrance into Nirvana, they preach the Law here on earth so that others may find the ford as well. Even the gods must bow before these mortals who have transcended the human condition.

Images of the Tirthankaras form the major part of Jaina art and are worshiped as examples of the perfection that man can attain. They remind worshipers of the virtues necessary for attaining Enlightenment and inspire the faithful to weave these qualities into their everyday lives.

Tirthankara images reflect the isolated, aloof nature of these perfected beings. They are immobile and without idiosyncrasies. Almost identical in appearance, only a few are recognizable as specific Tirthankaras. One of these is Rishabhanatha — sometimes called Adinatha — the first Tirthankara, who lived in mythical times (Figure 33). He is the only Tirthankara portrayed with the long, matted locks of an ascetic falling across his shoulders. Like other Tirthankaras, he is depicted naked, or sky-clad,[1] having abandoned all trappings of the physical world, and standing in meditation with feet apart and arms next to but not touching the body in the body-abandoning (*kayotsarga*) pose.

From the earliest period of Jaina art the Tirthankaras are depicted in a standardized form. This is evident when comparing the fourth-century image of Rishabhanatha (Figure 33) with a ninth-century image of Parshvanatha, the twenty-third Tirthankara

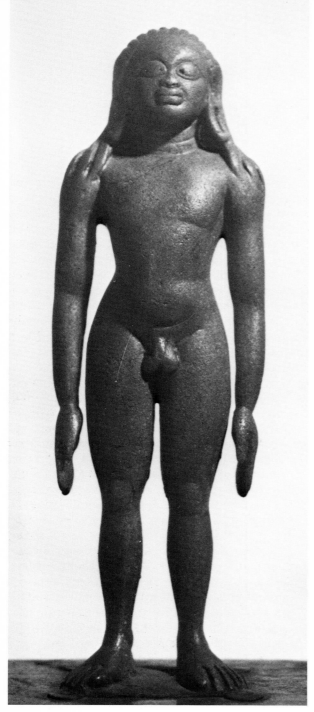

Figure 33. *Rishabhanatha.*
Bronze, H. 8⅝ inches.
India, Bihar, late Kushan Period, 4th century.
Patna Museum.

Figure 34. *Parshvanatha.*
Sandstone, H. 63¼ inches.
Central India, 9th century.
John L. Severance Fund CMA 61.419

52

(Figure 34). The latter also stands in the body-abandoning pose and is sky-clad. He bears on his chest a special diamond-shaped emblem, the *shrivatsa*, a small mark of sanctity borne only by Tirthankaras. Like many Tirthankara images, this one resembles Buddha images in a superficial way, having characteristics such as an *ushnisha*, three concentric beauty lines around the neck, and elongated earlobes (stretched by the weight of the jewels he wore as a young man), which are also *lakshanas*, or signs of the Buddha. The Buddha, however, is never shown in the body-abandoning pose and never bears the diamond-shaped *shrivatsa* on his chest. Most importantly, the Buddha is never depicted nude, but always wearing a monastic robe. He may seem sky-clad in some examples (for instance, Figure 24), but even here the edges of the Buddha's thin, clinging robe can be seen at his ankles, wrists, and shoulders.

Parshvanatha is another Tirthankara who, from the earliest period of Jaina art, is recognizable by a symbol or cognizance — multiple flaring serpent hoods sheltering his head. Serpents have long been revered in India. Cobras are prevalent there, and since time immemorial they have served as symbols of death (their bite can kill) and rebirth (they seem reborn when they shed their skin). Serpent deities (*nagas*) appear in every Indian religion: the Hindu gods Vishnu (Figures 5 and 7) and Shiva (Figures 13 and 14) are closely associated with them, and the Buddha is occasionally depicted with serpent hoods spread over his head since the Serpent King (*Nagaraja*) sheltered him from a storm in that fashion while the Buddha was meditating under the Bodhi Tree. Parshvanatha, before his own Enlightenment, had saved a family of serpents who were trapped in a burning log; he was able to perceive that there were serpents imprisoned in the fire because of his developing superior knowledge. Several years later, while practicing austerities, Par-

shvanatha was suddenly attacked by wild animals and a ferocious storm conjured up by a malevolent demon. Sensing Parshvanatha's plight, the great Serpent King (who in a previous life had been the serpent Parshvanatha had saved from a fire) coiled himself around the meditating ascetic's body to protect him from the beasts, and spread his multiple hoods over Parshvanatha's head to shelter him from the storm. In this sculpture (Figure 34), the endless coils of the Serpent King are visible behind the body of the Tirthankara; the heads of the Great Serpent have been broken off and only the multiple flared hoods encircling Parshvanatha's head remain.

Tirthankaras are also represented seated cross-legged in the usual yogic lotus position (Figure 35). The painting depicts Rishabhanatha in Heaven awaiting his final rebirth. Crowned and heavily jeweled in a manner befitting a future prince, he wears a white loincloth. The diamond-shaped *shrivatsa* on his chest indicates that he is also about to become a Tirthankara. Underneath his throne is the *dharmachakra*, the Wheel of the Law of both the Jaina and Buddhist faiths; on the front of his throne (just underneath his crossed ankles) is a tiny humped bull, Rishabhanatha's animal cognizance. Over the Tirthankara's head is an honorific parasol that resembles a stupa. It is flanked by two elephants with trunks upraised in the conventional position that signifies the sprinkling of water, a symbolic representation of fertilizing rainclouds and hence a symbol of general auspiciousness. In niches below the elephants are two heavenly musicians. Two *yakshas* stand in niches flanking Rishbhanatha.

Similar imagery surrounds the earlier Parshvanatha icon (Figure 34). Above the serpent hoods surrounding Parshvanatha's head are three ascending parasols reminiscent of the crowning element of a stupa mast (Figure 29); these honorific parasols are

Figure 35. *Rishabhanatha in Heaven.*
Color and gold on paper, $4^3/8$ x $10^3/16$ inches.
India, Western Gujarat, ca. 1500.
Gift of Mr. and Mrs. William E. Ward CMA 83.1047
In early Jaina art only two Tirthankaras were recognizable as individuals. In later times, each Tirthankara was assigned an animal symbol as identification. Rishabhanatha's animal is the bull, visible on the front of the throne just beneath his crossed ankles.

flanked by auspicious elephants and other attendants. The small figures on the sides of the stele are *nagini* (female serpent deities) carrying musical instruments. Two *yakshas* flank Parshvanatha's legs, and other *nagini* stand behind them.

These immovable images of the Jaina Tirthankaras effectively convey the singular perfection of these men who have won Nirvana through their own strenuous efforts and have been mentally and physically transformed by their hard-won Perfect Knowledge. Purged of all human idiosyncrasies, their bodies are immaculately pure. Their very sameness lends them an air of being beyond time, the conquerors (*jinas*) of *maya*.

The individual biographies of the twenty-four Tirthankaras are virtually interchangeable, differing only in the details of their mothers' prophetic dreams.

Essentially, a Tirthankara's earthly life parallels that of the historic Buddha, and in fact, the twenty-fourth (and last) Perfect Man — the only historic Tirthankara — was a contemporary of the Buddha Shakyamuni. His princely name was Vardhamana, but after he achieved the supreme human triumph of Enlightenment, he was known by the title Mahavira (Great Hero).

The biography of a Tirthakara begins in Heaven, where he awaits his last rebirth (Figure 35). Other frequently depicted Events of the Embryo include representations of the king and queen who will be his parents, his future mother lying on a couch in a pavilion, and symbols of her sixteen prophetic dreams. The Tirthankara's birth is illustrated by a woman holding a child while reclining on a couch. His renunciation of the world is depicted in several ways: giving away jewels,

Figure 36. *Mahavira's Samavasarna.*
Color and gold on paper, $4^{7}/_{16}$ x $10^{3}/_{16}$ inches.
India, Gujarat, 15th century.
Edward L. Whittmore Fund CMA 32.119/17
Mahavira's animal symbol is the lion.

leaving his palace on a palaquin, or an enclosed litter, carried by several men, or plucking out his hair — the beginning of his commitment to the extreme asceticism of the Jain faith. Like the Buddha, the Tirthankara achieves Enlightenment under a tree, thereby honoring the ancient tree-worshiping fertility cults of pre-Vedic India. The moment of his Enlightenment, a concept too abstract to convey visually, is implicit in the depictions of the Tirthankara preaching to the universe, the Jaina equivalent of the Buddha's First Sermon (Figure 36). In the center of the painting, the Tirthankara Mahavira sits in the usual yogic position. He is adorned with honorific jewels and bears the small diamond-shaped *shrivatsa* on his chest. Like Rishabhanatha (Figure 33), he wears a crown with two peculiar floral ornaments growing from it. This odd detail seems to be developed through the endless

repetitive depictions of curved branches bearing pendant leaves placed over an Enlightened One's head in both Jaina and Buddhist art, symbolizing the Tree of Enlightenment (Figure 22).

Mahavira sits in the middle of a *samavasarana* (Figure 36), a stadiumlike celestial preaching hall built by the gods for the sole purpose of hearing a Tirthankara preach immediately after his Enlightenment; a new *samavasarana* is built for each Tirthankara. The inner wall of the three-walled circular structure is made of jewels, the middle wall of gold, and the outer wall of silver. Gateways to the four cardinal directions pierce the walls. According to legend, gods, men, and beasts gather in the *samavasarana* to hear the Tirthankara preach. In this illustration, that universal audience is represented in part by a serpent and a mongoose near the top of the uppermost gate and, below them, a horse and a lion. Normally hostile to each other, these pairs of animals meet in the peaceful atmosphere engendered by the Tirthankara's preaching. Beneath the bottom gate is an elephant in the sprinkling-water pose; he is paired with a mythical, elephant-trunked lion.

Representations of a Tirthankara after his final death (the death itself is seldom, if ever, depicted) are identical to representations of a Tirthankara in Heaven (Figure 35) except for the addition of a thin, white crescent-moon form that stretches across the bottom of these small paintings. It represents the inverted parasol of pure white gold at the top of the universe, above which the released souls of Perfect Men (*Siddhas*) dwell in omniscience and bliss.

Conclusion

Images of these Tirthankaras and the stories of their lives are stereotyped and repetitive because the Tirthankaras are ultimately identical. They have each followed the same path to the same end; they are purged of their human (or even godlike) individuality and stand poised at the point of entering their final formless, eternal state. The meticulously regulated — even monotonous — iconography of Jaina art simply reinforces the Jaina belief that there is *one* path, and one path only, leading to eternal bliss: the painful, self-denying, non-violent path of the Tirthankaras.

Notes

*This fragment of verse is not found in all recensions of the *Kalakacaryakatha*, the legend of the sage Kalaka, but does form part of one of the oldest recensions, the Long Anonymous Version of the legend. See W. Norman Brown, *The Story of Kalaka*, Oriental Studies No. 1 (Washington: Freer Gallery of Art, 1933), p. 61.

[1] After the death of Mahavira, a contemporary of the Buddha and the last or twenty-fourth Tirthankara, his order of monks split into two factions. The most extreme group was called Digambara (sky-clad) since their self-denying ordinances forbade them even the wearing of clothes; the other order, less extreme in its interpretation of self-denial, was called Svetambara (white-robed). Since it was not a dispute over doctrine, the two groups eventually reunited. There are only a handful of sky-clad monks in India today.

Glossary

Aryan. The Indo-European nomadic tribes who invaded and settled India around 1500 BC.

Bhakti. The intense love of and devotion to god.

Bodhi. Wisdom, knowledge.

Brahmanism. The religion based on the Sanskrit texts known as the *Brahmanas* that set out the rationale and principles of an elaborate system of sacrifice. They are also commentaries on the earlier Vedic texts.

Brahmin. The priestly or sage caste.

Caste. See introduction.

Chakravartin. A turner of the wheel, a world emperor, a universal monarch.

Dharma. Law, universal order, duty, or doctrine.

Dhoti. A thin, wrapped and pleated skirt worn by both men and women in India.

Dravidian. The pre-Aryan or pre-Vedic culture of India; also a family of languages spoken in southern India.

Hinayana. Lesser Vehicle; an early monastic form of Buddhism.

Karma. The spiritual debt or gain accumulated by one's actions in previous lives which will bear fruit — for better or worse — in this life and/or the lives to come.

Kshatriya. The warrior or princely caste.

Lakshana. Mark or sign; one of the thirty-two auspicious marks distinguishing the anatomy of Buddha and sometimes the Tirthankaras.

Linga. A sign; a short, rounded pillar, emblematic of the Hindu god Shiva.

Mahapurusha. Great Man; the primordial cosmic man in Vedic mythology.

Mahayana. Greater Vehicle; later theistic form of Buddhism.

Mudra. Hand gesture conveying a specific meaning.

Naga. A serpent deity.

Nagini. A female serpent deity.

Nirvana. Extinction; escape from all forms of existence, freedom from rebirth.

Pali. The early Indian language in which the early Hinayana Buddhist scriptures were written.

Parinirvana. The final death, with no ensuing rebirth, of the historical Buddha at Kushinagara.

Sanskrit. The language of the Aryan conquerors of India, the classical language of ancient India.

Shakti. Energy; usually the female personification of a male god's energy.

Shudras. The laborer caste.

Stupa. A funeral mound, tumulus.

Theravada. Teaching of the Elders; the early monastic Buddhism also known as Hinayana.

Transmigration. The concept that the soul is subject to continuous rebirth.

Tushita Heaven. The Heaven of the Thirty-Three Gods, the heavenly residence of the Historical Buddha before his last birth on earth; also the heavenly residence of Maitreya, the Buddha of the Future.

Urna. A tuft of hair between the eyebrows; an auspicious mark of a Buddha or Tirthankara.

Ushnisha. A cranial protuberance, an auspicious mark of a Buddha or Tirthankara, symbolizing supreme knowledge.

Vaishya. The merchant caste.

Veda. Knowledge; the four ancient Indian books known as the Vedas are the *Rig-Veda*, *Yajur-Veda*, *Sama-Veda*, and *Atharva-Veda*. These texts date to the period between the end of the Indus Valley culture and the life of the historical Buddha, or about 1500-500 BC. They are the basis of the early Brahmanic religion of India, and are revered as the earliest sacred texts of Hinduism.

Yaksha. The male companion of a female Yakshi.

Yakshi. A female fertility deity or tree spirit of pre-Vedic India.

Yoga. Yoking together; the suppression through progressive discipline of all activity of the body, mind, and individual will in order to attain both liberation from all pain and suffering, and reintegration with the eternal and measureless cosmos (that is, Nirvana, or union with the Absolute).

Selected Bibliography

Brown, W. Norman. *The Story of Kalaka*. Oriental Studies, no. 1. Washington: Freer Gallery of Art, 1933.

Conze, Edward. *Buddhism: Its Essence and Development*. Magnolia, MA: Peter Smith, 1959.

Cowell, E. B., trans. *The Buddha-Karita of Asvaghosha*. Buddhist Mahayana Texts, pt. 1. Oxford: The Clarendon Press, 1894; reprint, New York: Dover Publications, 1969.

Cummings, Mary. *The Lives of the Buddha in the Art and Literature of Asia*. Michigan Papers on South and Southeast Asia, no. 20. Ann Arbor: The University of Michigan, Center for South and Southeast Asian Studies, 1982.

Danielou, Alain. *Hindu Polytheism*. London: Routledge and Kegan Paul, 1964.

Davids, T. W. Rhys, trans. *The Maha-parinibbana Suttanta in Buddhist Suttas*. Oxford: Clarendon Press, 1881; reprint, New York: Dover Publications, 1969.

Dimmitt, Cornelia, and J. A. B. van Buitenen, eds. and trans. *Classical Hindu Mythology: A Reader in the Sanskrit Puranas*. Philadelphia: Temple University Press, 1978.

Dye, Joseph M. *Ways to Shiva: Life and Ritual in Hindu India*. Philadelphia: Philadelphia Museum of Art, 1980.

Foucher, Alfred C. A. *The Life of the Buddha According to Ancient Texts and Monuments*. Abridged and translated by Simone Brangier Boas. Middletown, CT: Wesleyan University Press, 1963.

Gupta, Shakti Madan. *Vishnu and His Incarnations*. Bombay, New Delhi: Somaiya Publications, 1974.

Gupte, Ramesh Shankar. *Iconography of the Hindus, Buddhists, and Jains*. Bombay: D. B. Taraporevala Sons, 1972.

Ingalls, Daniel H. H., trans. *Sanskrit Poetry from Vidyakara's "Treasury."* 2nd printing. Cambridge, MA: Harvard University Press, 1972.

Jain, Jyotindra, and Eberhard Fischer. *Jaina Iconography*. Parts 1 and 2. Iconography of Religions, Sec. XIII, fasc. 12, Leiden: E. J. Brill, 1978.

Kalupahana, David J., and Indrani Kalupahana. *The Way of Siddhartha: A Life of the Buddha*. Boulder and London: Shambhala Publications, 1982.

Kramrisch, Stella. *Manifestations of Shiva*. Philadelphia: Philadelphia Museum of Art, 1981.

Krishna, Nanditha. *The Art and Iconography of Vishnu-Narayana*. Bombay: D. B. Taraporevala Sons, 1980.

Michell, George. *The Hindu Temple: An Introduction to Its Meaning and Form*. London: Paul Elek, 1977.

Muir, John, trans., ed., and comp. *Original Sanskrit Texts on the Origin and History of the People of India, Their Religions and Institutions*. Vol. 4, *Comparison of the Vedic with the Later Representations of the Principal Indian Deities*. 2d ed. rev. Amsterdam: Oriental Press, 1967.

Müller, F. Max, trans. *The Upanishads*. 2 vols. The Sacred Books of the East, vols. 1, 15. Oxford: Clarendon Press, 1879-1900.

Pal, Pratapaditya, with Robert L. Brown. *Light of Asia: Buddha Sakyamuni in Asian Art*. Los Angeles: Los Angeles County Museum of Art, 1984.

Pargiter, F. Eden, trans. *Markandeya Purana*. Calcutta: The Asiatic Society of Bengal, 1904; New Delhi: Varanasi, Indological Book House, 1969.

Prabhavananda, Swami, and Christopher Isherwood, trans. *Bhagavad-Gita: The Song of God*. New York: Mentor Books, New American Library, 1951.

Rapson, Edward James, ed. *The Cambridge History of India. Vol. 1,* Ancient India. Cambridge: University Press, 1922.

Rowland, Benjamin. *The Art and Architecture of India: Buddhist, Hindu, Jain*. The Pelican History of Art. London, Baltimore, Melbourne: Penguin Books, 1953.

Shah, Umakant P. *Studies in Jaina Art*. Banaras: Jaina Cultural Research Society, 1955.

Snellgrove, David L., ed. *The Image of the Buddha*. Paris: UNESCO; New York: Kodansha, 1978.

Thapar, Romila. *A History of India*. Vol. 1. London, Baltimore, Melbourne: Penguin Books, 1966.

Thomas, P. *Epics, Myths, and Legends of India, A Comprehensive Survey of the Sacred Lore of the Hindus, Buddhists, and Jains*. Bombay: D. B. Taraporevala Sons, 1958.

Zimmer, Heinrich Robert. *The Art of Indian Asia: Its Mythology and Transformations*. Completed and edited by Joseph Campbell. 2 vols. The Bollingen Series no. 39. New York: Pantheon Books, 1955.

—. *Myths and Symbols in Indian Art and Civilization*. Edited by Joseph Campbell. Bollingen Series 6. New York: Pantheon Books, 1946.

BL2001.2
B64
1985

PITT OCLC

MA